Hundred roses for one butterfly

VERY SHORT POEMS

ORIGINAL ARABIC TEXTS AND ENGLISH TRANSLATION

Fethi Sassi

Cyberwit.net
HIG 45 Kaushambi Kunj, Kalindipuram
Allahabad - 211011 (U.P.) India
http://www.cyberwit.net
Tel: +(91) 9415091004 +(91) (532) 2552257
E-mail: info@cyberwit.net

Printed at Repro India Limited.

DEDICACE

" I dreamt that I write like Kafka "

(Marquez)

O; poet !
write a poem, and then go sign between words.

A bird sings on the tree;
the cloud is hiding in the sky.

The balcony shames the morning's face.

On my balcony;
meet the birds to read a poem.

Try to create me again,
from your hands' clay.

A flash;
I become in the dimness of your absence.

But,
poetry is your absence in the moment of sunset .

I am afraid that I miss you;
and I become a pain.

Too much you are,
and I am few in a poem.

Whenever I kiss you,
sprung on my fingers a tale.

In the moment of your absence;
the crying surrounds me.

Crowded with absence;
are your lips.

Every riddle that I used in the instant of your absence,
proved my fail.

I vowed your eyes to passion,
Isn't this prayer enough for you ?

How do they play this music;
and they don't know your eyes !

Look,
how many butterflies fly
above this poem ?

A pot thinks:
(from where this garden can be kissed ?)

The absence,
Is the rhythm of your face in the exile.

This look,
is a morning without questions.

Who is this star ?
overlooking my balcony .

I am afraid to say : I love you ;
and the trees hear me.

We were two clouds apart.
and we were separated.

The moon came whispering to the water.
The cloud didn't hear anything.

As the cloud taste,
I flew, and I planted you in my relief.

They spotted me on the sly.
When I was hanging out, dawn in her eyes.

I kiss you;
and I am saying: the first drop is a kiss.

I wasn't there,
I was over a cloud catching dew.

Wake up;
the talks are sleeping on her lips.

My longing to you melted all the salt of my poems.

When I touch you; my fingertips rain poetry .

Was your absence sufficient to all this presence ?

I ran from you,
and I forgot you live in me.

I wore perfume.
than jasmine got high.

Hand me a bit of fragrance,
so I flirt with the spring.

Who else but me,
will embay your cheeks with saliva sunset.

She was flying;
above the poem's butterfly.
Drinking a grain.

Windless night;
on the mouth of the tree.
A sigh of passion.

Lying ,
under a tree,
and my fingers caresses the dew.

Storms of scent,
made of her fragrance.

When you leave,
I will wash up with the water of absence.

This poetry tortures me…
Bleeding line after line

Why whenever we are together;
we become one?

Your kisses on my body,
are a ticking bomb.

Whenever I miss your perfume.
I praise on behalf of all roses.

I open the window on her face.
and the appeal amazes me.

I found you a wandering letter in a poem.

May the night bend,
when her shadow comes.

Give me your face,
to write down all my poems .

I rush to the door, and I leave it open.
So the night goes out.

I want to write a poem, in the edge of her face.

Is your face enough,
to sew all my disappointments?

It's like you are a flock of pigeons that lures me
to the flames.

Show me your face, so I do not blame the mirror.

How could the flower be ashamed of her perfume;
and veil ?

Come closer,
to fall from you.

Of shyness;
blossoms the flower,
before she sends a speech to her beloved.

Who triggered the shy night in your eyes ?

We write, as like as the clouds.

Here I am dwelling a rose; and justifying a rose.

How all this spray fell from your eyes
??

How beautiful the damage is in your presence !

With you; all the road lead to you.

The smell of the coffee on your lips,
and your tongue is a waiter.

Go a little bit far, to see you more beautiful.

If you leave, I will breath your name.

What am I seeing ?
my hanged poems in your eyes.

Grapes of water nourish the wounds of distance.

The stars are wooding early, for the chilly nights.

The moon is trilling in the sky, a wedding of a star.

The moon winking to a star;
making the night angry.

My face in the mirror.
Is a coming confusion.

Of the weight of loss,
I break the glass of my waiting.

A violin is singing;
its voice is an orphan night.

On her cheeks,
rests a pregnant mole.

In the sky,
the moon is looking for a question of the darkness.

A silly night,
revealed its secrets to a cloud.

My sweetheart,
I peel her , and she wets me.

I am a travelling bird;
but I am shy of the sky.

I crave to this thirst in your eyes.

Could this world fit in only one poem ?

I found her, when I was looking for other things.

The night is a swimming ink in the darkness.

To write poetry is to wipe the dust on languages.

A bird standing on a tree;
sending his wings to the horizon.

I seek refuge in your face from my sad poems.

On the stairs of dream , I rise up to the sky,
the moon is waiting for me.

Whenever I sleep with my language ,
I gave birth to a poem.

In the pond of passion we rose up,
and we wiped our wounds.

The moon is lonely tonight, who shines its pillow ?

Birds in the horizon; the sky is a tree.

We are all spilling tonight, in the cup .of the night talks.

A star in the sky, is a waiting bride.

The sky has forgotten its fingertips, hanging in an inkwell.

Stars are flirting with each other, the moon is sad.

The nights of winter; are wet sorrows.

The moon is observing his face in the water.
The universe is sweating.

A lonely candle in the dark.
The light is worried.

The ax cuts the tree.
The bird is crying.

At the night of my birthday;
the candles are flirting.

How did you become all the beaches,
and I became the oyster!

You are gone; and you left a chaotic perfume on my cheeks.

Whenever I wrote you a poem;
all languages cry.

Biography of FETHI SASSI

Poet, translator,

Born in the city of Nabeul , Tunisia (1962), **Fethi Sassi** completed his elementary school in Sousse. Later he continued his studies at the technical school in Sousse completed till the baccalaureate after he stops his study in the purpose to help his family. He completed his graduate studies at the Free University Ariana, Tunisia, specializing in International business Studies. He has in fact decided to stop to the primary degree to begin the commercial work. Fethi Sassi did a long period in the commercial business. And he was active in his personal literary life. For many years he has written poetry, proses, essays. He is a regular contributor to many magazines, in Tunisia and abroad, writing on many cultural and literary topics, especially concerning poetry. Fethi Sassi became well known in Sousse after the publication of his first book entitled: (A seed of love) published in 2010. Later he published a number of other books. His poems are translated in more ten languages and published in several international Literature Anthologies. He is the most translated Tunisian Poet and well known in Europe. According to a number of literary critics, he is the genuine representative of modern Tunisian poetry. International critics and poets wrote for him a lot of articles considering him as great Tunisian poet. He is a member of many international poetry clubs and Is a contributor to many literary and cultural magazines, especially in English; a member of the union of Tunisian writers. and the literary club of the culture house in Sousse .The wisdom of his work in the field of Literature is based in the attention that he pays to the poetic expression, modern exploration of the text and the depth of the message. His Genre is focused more on love lyrics and elliptical verse intertwined with metaphors and artistic symbolism and surrealism pictures. Currently resides and works in Sousse, Tunisia.

Published works:
1. "A seed of love" 2010 (poetry)
2. "I dream… and I sign on birds the last dreams" 2013 (poetry)
3. "A sky for a strange bird", 2016 (poetry) second edition 2018
4. "As a lonely rose on a chair" 2017 (poetry)
5. "I used to hang my face behind the door" 2018 (poetry)
6. "A new method for absence" 2019 (poetry).

Arabic Books of Fethi Sassi translated by Fethi Sassi
1. Translated short poetry book published in Canada, translated from Arabic to English (And you are the entire poem) 2017.
2. Translated short poetry book published in Canada, translated from Arabic to English (Wings and Butterflies) 2018.
3. Translated poetry book published in Zimbabwe (I throw a star in a wine glass) translated from Arabic to English 2018.
4. Translated poetry Arabic book to English published in Canada (I used to hang my face behind the door) 2019.

English books translated to Arabic by Fethi Sassi

1. Translated poetry book published in Egypt translated from English to Arabic of the great Turkish poetess (Poems to the shadows) 2017.
2. Translated poetry book published in Egypt translated from English to Arabic of the great Greek poet (Odes to Aphrodite) 2017.

3. Translated poetry book published in USA translated with 5 other translator To many languages of the American poet S.Bohen (God's silence a lion's roar)

My books Translated to other languages

1.Translated the third poetry book (Ciel pour un oiseau étranger) by the Moroccan academic translator M.Serhani published by l' Harmatton house in France in 2018.

2.Translated poetry book to the French and English (All the universe is the face of my beloved) 2018.

CONTACT

https://www.facebook.com/fethi.sassi.54

MEMBER IN IWA

http://www.iwabogdani.org/home/